EAST

SUSHIMANIA

EAST

SUSHIMANIA

UMSCHAU

EAST

Sushi kommt aus Japan. Folglich sind Asiaten, die an einer Sushibar meisterhaft und kunstvoll mit ihren scharfen Messern Sushi und Sashimi zubereiten, ausschließlich Japaner. Doch weder das eine noch das andere ist richtig. Es ist zwar nicht mit Sicherheit zu sagen, wo genau Sushi erfunden wurde. Aber man weiß, dass man bereits im alten China mit Essig gewürzten Reis für die Konservierung von Fisch verwendete. So bedeuten die beiden chinesischen Schriftzeichen für Sushi im weitesten Sinne „konservierter Fisch". Irgendwann stellte man fest, dass die Kombination aus gewürztem Reis und Fisch sehr gut schmeckt. Das war die Vorstufe des heute bekannten Sushi. Vermutlich kam diese durch Zufall entstandene kulinarische Kreation zusammen mit dem Reisanbau im vierten vorchristlichen Jahrhundert nach Japan, und ohne Zweifel haben Japaner die feine Speise mit Reis, Fisch (roh, gekocht oder mariniert), Meeresfrüchten oder Gemüse perfektioniert. Doch Sushi-Meister kommen auch aus anderen Ländern. Beste Beispiele sind die beiden Meister des *east*, die täglich ihre Gäste mit erlesenen Sushi-Spezialitäten erfreuen. Und sie sind dem Ursprungsland des Sushi näher als ein Japaner. Denn Tamatsu Tashi kommt aus Tibet, Ngima Sherpa aus Nepal. Gelernt haben beide ihr Handwerk aber auf klassischem Wege. Fast jedenfalls.

Tamatsu Tashi absolvierte seine ersten Lehrjahre bei seinem Vater, der am Jangtse direkt an der Grenze zu China ein kleines Restaurant besaß. „Wir Tibeter essen ja eigentlich keinen Fisch", sagt der 1973 geborene Tashi. „Aber die Chinesen sind ein großer Freund davon." So verkaufte sein Vater die Fischgerichte vor allem an die Chinesen jenseits des Flusses und brachte seinem Sohn den sorgfältigen Umgang mit Fisch bei. Tamatsu Tashi arbeitete in den folgenden Jahren in verschiedenen chinesischen Restaurants und machte die klassische Ausbildung eines angehenden Sushi-Meisters, die bis zu zehn Jahre dauern kann. Geduld ist dabei eine wichtige Tugend, denn mit Fisch kommt man in den ersten Jahren kaum in Berührung. Die Grundlage der Ausbildung ist nämlich zunächst: die Küche reinzuhalten, und dazu gehören auch Tellerwaschen und Bodenschrubben. Da der Reis entscheidend zum Geschmackserlebnis von Sushi beiträgt, ist das Reiskochen eine eigene Disziplin, mit der man sich als Lehrling ebenfalls mehrere Jahre beschäftigen muss. Das richtige Mischverhältnis von Reis, Essig, Zucker und Salz und die verschiedenen Garmethoden wollen gelernt sein. 2001 kam Tamatsu Tashi mit seiner Frau Dolma nach Deutschland und arbeitete mehrere Jahre in Würzburg bei dem mehrmals ausgezeichneten Sushi-Meister Kikuchi, bevor sie weiter an die „Waterkant" zogen.

Bevor Ngima Sherpa Hand an den Fisch legte, arbeitete er als Bergführer im nepalesischen Solukhumbu, einer Region des Himalaya im Nordosten Nepals an der Grenze zu Tibet. An dessen nördlichen Ausläufer steht der Mount Everest. Sherpa war bewusst, dass Bergsteigen zwar seine Leidenschaft, nichts aber für die Ewigkeit ist. Er besuchte seinen Onkel in Singapur, der dort ein Restaurant besitzt. Der 1977 geborene Nepalese fand Gefallen an der neuen Herausforderung, besonders an der Ausbildung zum Sushi-Meister. „Sushi forderte von Anfang an meine Kreativität heraus", erzählt Sherpa. „Diese traditionelle asiatische Speise neu zu definieren, zu variieren und zu verbessern, macht großen Spaß, bis heute." Nach drei Jahren kehrte er nach Nepal zurück, doch eine Liebe zog ihn im Jahr 2000 nach Hamburg. In der Hansestadt prägte er einige Jahre als Sushi-Meister entscheidend den Stil und Ruf des Restaurants von Steffen Henssler.

Seit 2008 nun führen Ngima Sherpa und Tamatsu Tashi die Sushibar im *east* und entwickeln stets neue Kreationen und Konzepte, das also, was man in der modernen

sushi comes from Japan. One would imagine, that Asians who expertly and artistically prepare the sushi and Sashimi with sharp knives at the sushi-bar are exclusively Japanese. Neither one nor the other statement is true. In fact it is not possible to say with any degree of certainty where exactly sushi was invented, but we do know that in ancient China rice spiced with vinegar was used to conserve fish. The meaning of the two Chinese characters for sushi in the widest sense is „conserved fish". At some point people realized that the combination of spiced rice and fish tastes really good. That was the preliminary stage of what is known as sushi today. Apparently this accidental culinary creation was brought to Japan together with the cultivation of rice in the 4th century, and without any doubt the Japanese perfected the delicious dish with rice, fish (raw, cooked or marinated) and seafood or vegetables. However, sushi masters also come from other countries. The best examples are the two masters of the *east*, who daily delight their guests with selected sushi specialties. And they are closer to sushi's country of origin than the Japanese, since Tamatsu Tashi is from Tibet, and Ngima Sherpa from Nepal. Both of them learned their trade in the classical manner. Well, almost.

Tamatsu Tashi passed his first years of study with his father, who owned a small restaurant at the Yangtze river, directly on the border with China. „Actually we Tibetans don't eat fish" says 37 year old Tashi, „but the Chinese are very fond of it." So, his father sold fish dishes for the most part to the Chinese on the other side of the river and taught his son the painstaking art of handling fish. In the following years Tamatsu Tashi worked at various Chinese restaurants and received the classic training of a future sushi master, which can last up to ten years. Therefore, having patience is an important virtue, because in the first years you actually come into very little contact with fish. Keeping the kitchen clean is above all the basic foundation of the initial training, which includes washing dishes and scrubbing floors. And since rice plays such a decisive role in the sushi taste experience, its preparation is a special discipline, which likewise will occupy the apprentice for a number of years. The proper mixture of rice, vinegar, sugar and salt and the various cooking methods employed, have to be learned. In 2001, Tamatsu Tashi and his wife Dolma came to Germany and worked for several years in Wurzburg with the multi award winning sushi master Kikuchi, before they moved up north to the coast.

Before Ngima Sherpa ever laid a hand on fish he worked as a mountain guide in Solukhumbu, a Nepalese region of the Himalayas in the Northeast on the Tibetan border. Along its northern foothills stands Mount Everest. Sherpa understood, that mountain climbing was his passion, but it wasn't something that he could do forever. He visited his uncle in Singapore who owned a restaurant there. Born in 1977, the Nepalese welcomed the new challenge, particularly the training he underwent to become a sushi master. „From the very beginning sushi drew out my creativity" says Sherpa. „To this day I enjoy to re-define these traditional Asian dishes, to introduce variations and improvements." After three years he returned to Nepal, but a love affair drew him back to Hamburg in 2000. As a sushi master he set the style and reputation of Steffen Henssler's restaurant in the Hanseatic city for several years.

Since 2008 Ngima Sherpa and Tamatsu Tashi have been running the Sushi bar at the *east* and are continually developing new creations and concepts, everything that in modern cuisine can be referred to as cross-over: The combination of Asian ingre-

Küche als Cross-Over bezeichnet: Die Kombination asiatischer Zutaten und Kochtraditionen mit europäischen Noten. Vor allem raffinierte Saucen haben sie entwickelt, mal mit brauner Butter experimentiert, alten Balsamico über Sashimi geträufelt, Schaum in eine Rolle fließen lassen. Die beiden Meister zelebrieren ihr Handwerk, und es macht ihnen Spaß. „Natürlich ist Sushi ein bisschen wie Fast-Food", schmunzelt Sherpa. „Aber ein sehr hochwertiges Fast-Food. Und es liegt an jedem selbst, sich dafür Zeit zu lassen und es zu genießen." Im *east* hat man dafür alle Zeit der Welt.
Sherpa und Tashi pflegen zudem, ganz in der Tradition eines Sushi-Meisters, Rituale. Dazu gehören ihre persönlichen, besonders scharfen Messer. „Nein", sagt der stets gut gelaunte Tashi, „ich verwende kein japanisches Messer. Die besten kommen aus Deutschland!" Die Messer sind namentlich gekennzeichnet, „denn jedes Messer hat seinen eigenen Stil", erklärt Sherpa, „hat man seinen gefunden, gibt man das Messer im wahrsten Sinne des Wortes nicht mehr aus der Hand."

Dem Meister vertrauen

Entscheidend für höchsten Genuss sind erlesene Zutaten. Und so werden auch ins *east* nur Fisch und Meeresfrüchte von bester Qualität und stets frisch geliefert, in Hamburg sitzt man natürlich an einer sehr guten Quelle. Am frischesten ist Fisch, wenn er nahezu geruchlos ist, das Fleisch fest, die Augen klar und die Kiemen tiefrot sind. Am beliebtesten sind Lachs und Thunfisch – vor allem der fettere und geschmacklich beste Thunfischbauch (Toro) – aber auch junger Gelbschwanz (Hamachi), Meerbrassen, Wolfsbarsch und Steinbutt, Tintenfisch, Oktopus, Makrelen, Aal, Muscheln und Seeigel, Hummer-, Langusten- und Krabbenfleisch, Garnelen und Kaisergranat, Rogen vom Lachs oder Fliegenfisch, im Grunde genommen alles, was das Meer hergibt, der Phantasie sind kaum Grenzen gesetzt. „Außerdem", darauf legen beide Sushi-Meister großen Wert, „müssen Sushis immer frisch gerollt sein, dann ist der Genuss am größten."
Es hat Tradition, vor allem in der gehobenen Gastronomie, dass die Sushi-Meister die einzelnen Sushis perfekt würzen; es muss eigentlich nicht mehr nachgewürzt werden, auch nicht mit Sojasauce oder Wasabi. „Aber", schränkt Ngima Sherpa ein, „das ist manchmal schwer zu vermitteln. Die meisten Gäste glauben, dass das Tunken in Sauce und Wasabi einfach dazu gehört. Doch Sojasauce ist intensiv und verdeckt oftmals den besonderen Geschmack des Fisches." Man sollte also den Meistern vertrauen. Möchte man auf Sojasauce aber nicht verzichten, sollte man zumindest dies beachten: Man taucht die Fischseite in die Sojasauce, nicht die Reisseite! „Und möchte man Sushi auf ganz traditionelle Weise essen", ergänzt Tamatsu Tashi, „dann nimmt man die Finger, nicht die Stäbchen." Und Gari, eingelegten Ingwer, isst man zwischen den einzelnen Sushis, um den Geschmack der verschiedenen Fische auf der Zunge und im Gaumen zu neutralisieren.
Und was essen die Meister selbst am liebsten? „Nun", sagt Ngima Sherpa, „ich bin ein großer Fan der deftigeren Küche: Schnitzel, Rinderrouladen oder Gulasch, wunderbar!" Tamatsu Tashi hingegen kann sich mit der europäischen Küche nicht besonders anfreunden. „Sie ist mir zu fleischlastig", gesteht der Tibeter. Also kocht er zusammen mit seiner Frau Dorma vor allem indisch, tibetisch oder nepalesisch, mit vielen frischen Kräutern. „Aber es gibt auch ab und an eine Ausnahme", lacht Tashi. „Meine Frau tischt dann doch gerne Klöße, Rotkohl oder Braten auf" – seine Frau hat in Würzburg in einem bayerischen Restaurant gearbeitet. Auch das ist Cross-Over.

dients and cooking traditions along with a distinctive European character. Above all, they've developed ingenious sauces, sometimes experimenting with brown butter, sprinkling old balsamic vinegar over Sashimi, or pouring foam into a roll. Both of the masters celebrate their skills, and they have a lot of fun doing it. „Sure, sushi is a little bit like fast-food", says Sherpa, with a smile. „But very high quality fast-food. And it's up to each person to take the time and enjoy it." In the *east* you can take all the time you want.
Adhering to the tradition of a sushi master, Sherpa and Tashi cultivate a sense of ritual. And their personal razor sharp knives are an integral part of that tradition. „No," says the always good humored Tashi, „I don't use a Japanese knife. The best ones are made in Germany!" The knives are initialed with the name of the owner, „because every knife has its own style", explains Sherpa „once you've found yours, you never let it out of your hands, in the truest sense of the word."

Trust the Master

To attain the greatest pleasure, quality ingredients are essential. And so only fish and other seafood of the best quality are always freshly delivered to the *east* – Hamburg, of course, providing the ideal source. Fish are at their freshest, when they are practically odorless, the meat is firm, the eyes clear and the gills are of a deep red. The best liked are salmon and tuna fish – above all the more fatty and most flavorful stomach (Toro) of the tuna fish, but also young yellowtail (Hamachi), sea breen, sea bass, turbot, cuttlefish, octopus, mackarel, eel, mussels, sea urchin, lobster, spiny lobster and crab meet, shrimps and Dublin bay prawn, fish eggs from salmon or fly fish – basically everything the sea offers, the only limit is your imagination. „Apart from that," and that is where both sushi masters place the greatest value, „Sushi must be always freshly rolled, to attain the greatest pleasure."
It's a tradition, above all in upscale gastronomy, that the sushi master's sushi is perfectly spiced; there is actually no necessity to add any more spices, not even soy sauce or wasabi. „But," Ngima Sherpa admits, „that's sometimes hard to get across. Most guests believe that dipping sushi into soy sauce and wasabi is part of it. But in fact, soy sauce is very intense and often dominates the taste of the fish." One should trust the masters after all. But if you don't want to do without soy sauce, you should at least pay attention to the following advice: Dip the fish side into the soy sauce, not the rice side! „And if you want to eat sushi the traditional way", adds Tamatsu Tashi, „you use your fingers and not chopsticks." And Gari, the pickled ginger, is eaten in between the individual sushi to neutralize the taste of the various fish on the tongue and the palate.
And what is the master's favorite dish? „Now," says Ngima Sherpa, „I'm a big fan of a hearty kitchen: Schnitzel, Beef roulade or Goulash, wonderful!" Whereas Tamatsu Tashi is not a friend of the European kitchen. „It's too meat oriented for my taste," confesses the Tibetan. With his wife Durma he cooks Indian, Tibetan or Nepalese, with a lot of fresh herbs. „But there are of course exceptions," Tashi laughs. „My wife serves dumplings, red cabbage or roast," – his wife worked in Wurzburg in a Bavarian restaurant. Another example of cross-over.

Super Crunchy Roll

Salmon Gold

Kohl Roll

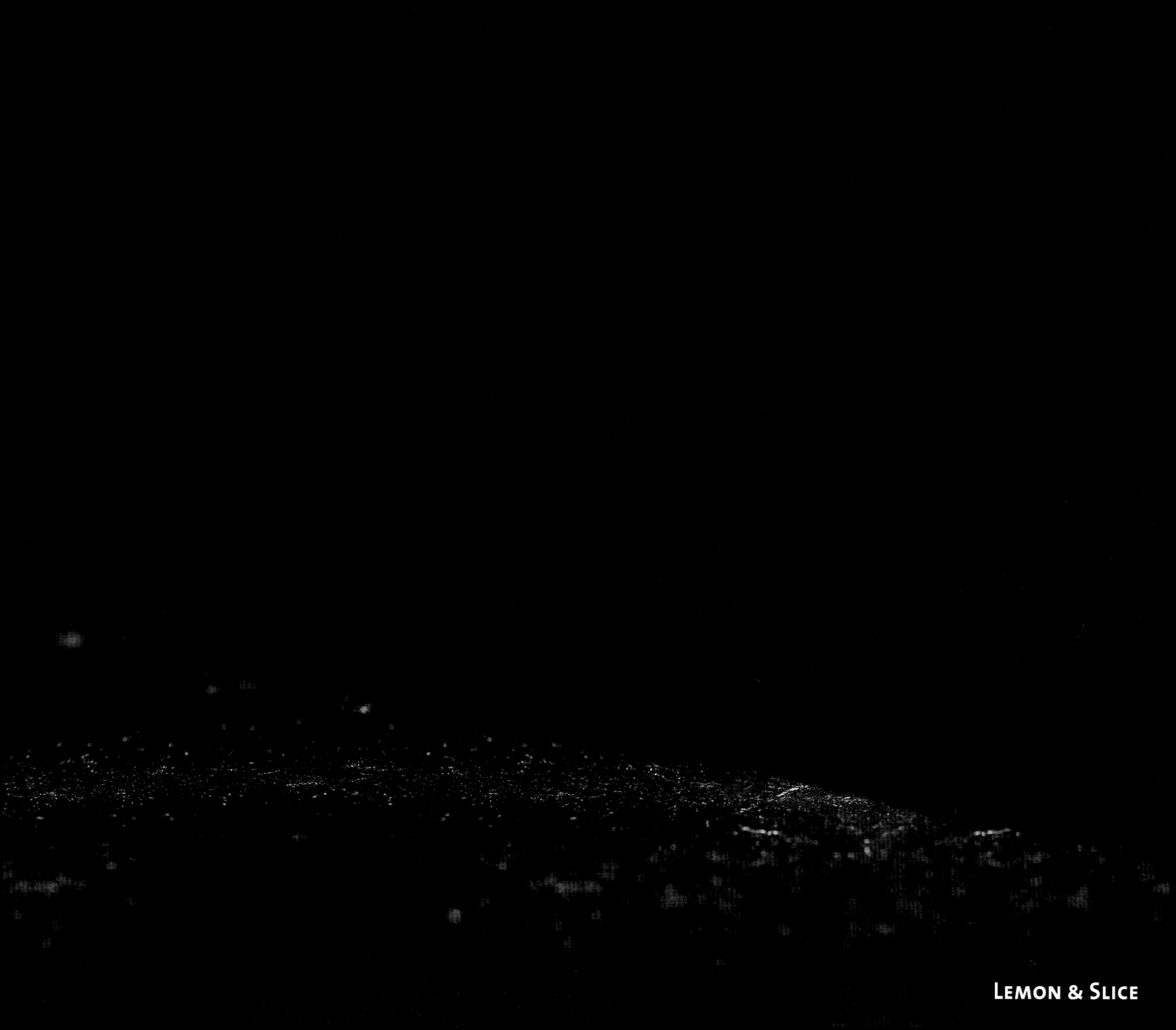
Lemon & Slice

Beef Tataki

SALMON DREAM ROLL

East California Roll

Lobster Roll

CRISPY IKARIMI-LACHS

TURBOT BLACK & WHITE

Duck-Tower

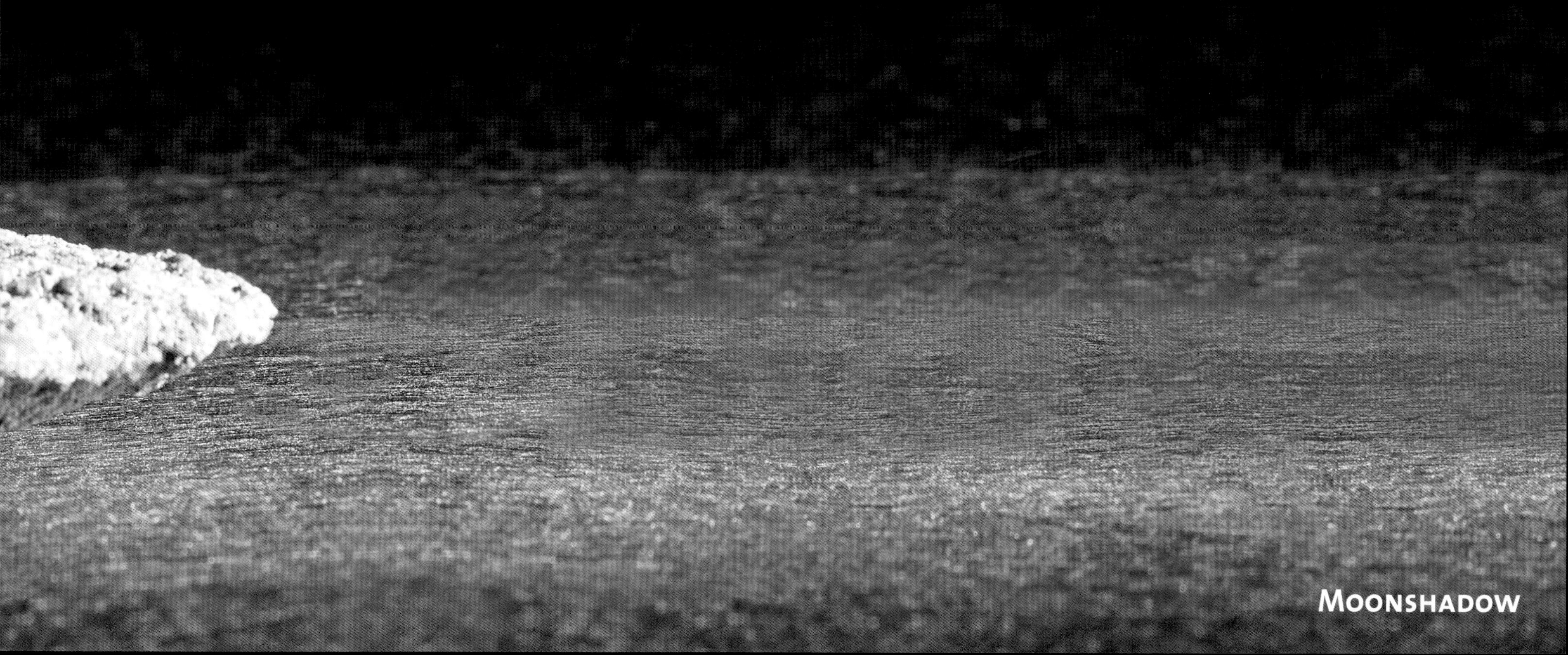
MOONSHADOW

Sliced Octopus

KING'S SASHIMI

White Dream Roll

Spicy Rabbit Tiger Roll

Double-Smoke-Unagi Roll

Loup de Green Roll

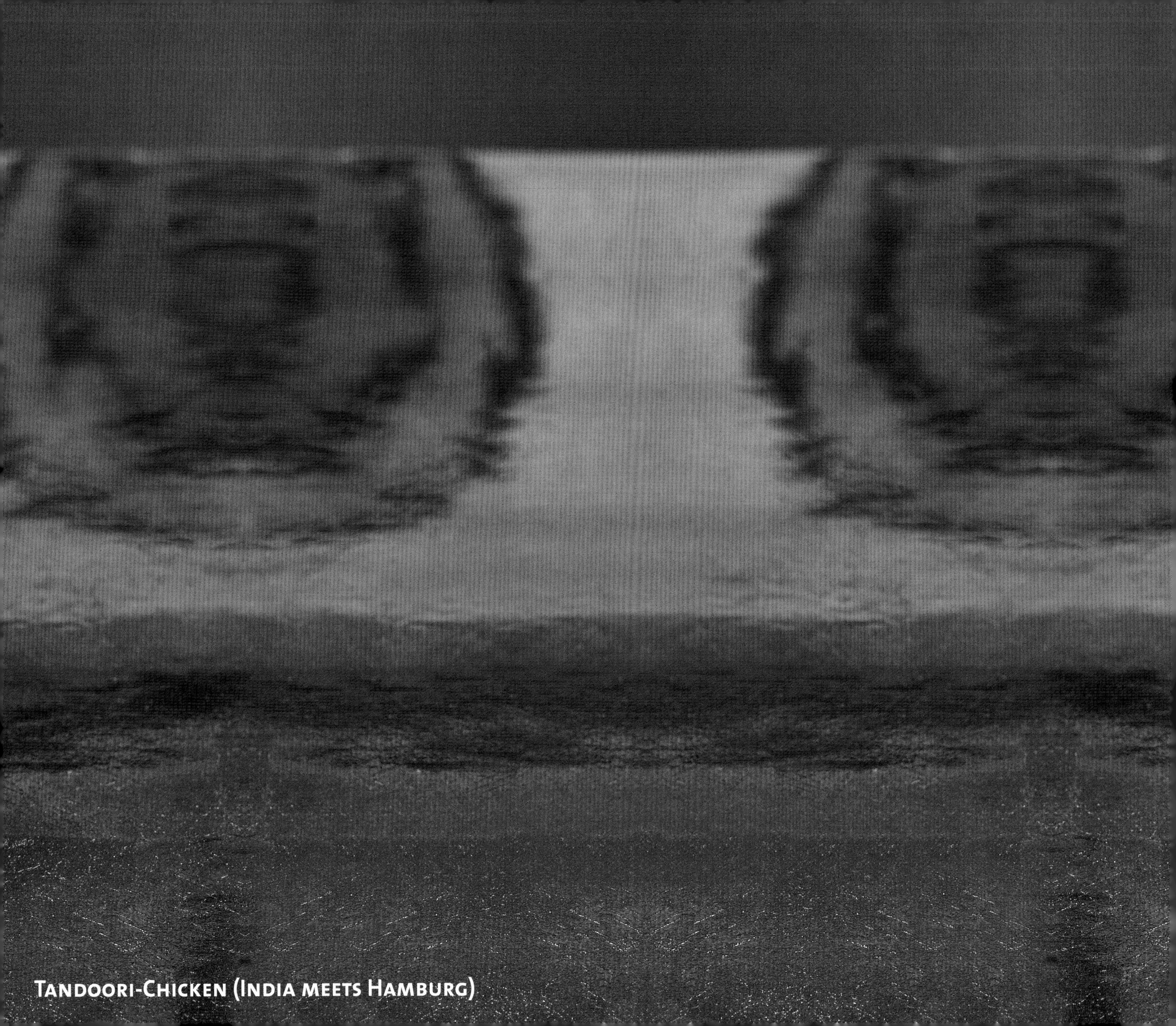

Tandoori-Chicken (India meets Hamburg)

Wooden Cucumber Tuna Sashimi

Sweet Crab Roll on Mozer's

Tobiko Point

Racasse Sashimi

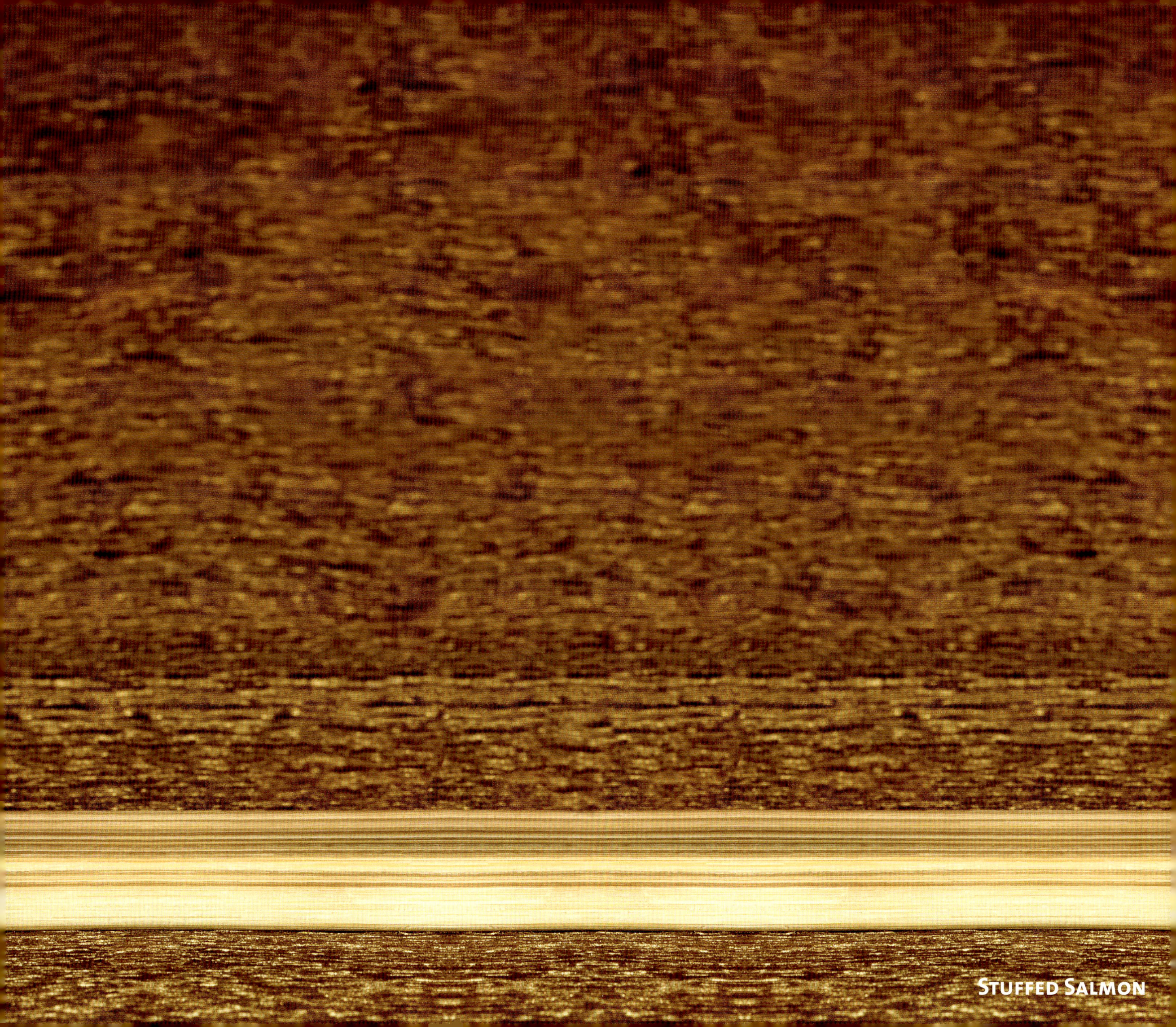
STUFFED SALMON

Naked Salmon

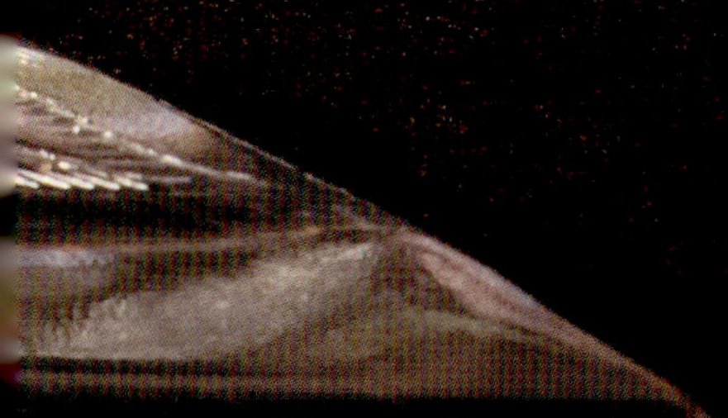

Khukuri Eel

Mister Beef Roll

Imprisoned Salmon Sashimi

Deep Sea Roll

Rabbit-Sushi

Watermelon Jacob

Black Tuna on Green

Salmon Dream Sashimi

MILA RAPER

Khampa-Beef-Sashimi

Crazy Daisy Duck Roll

Brushed Mint-Chicken

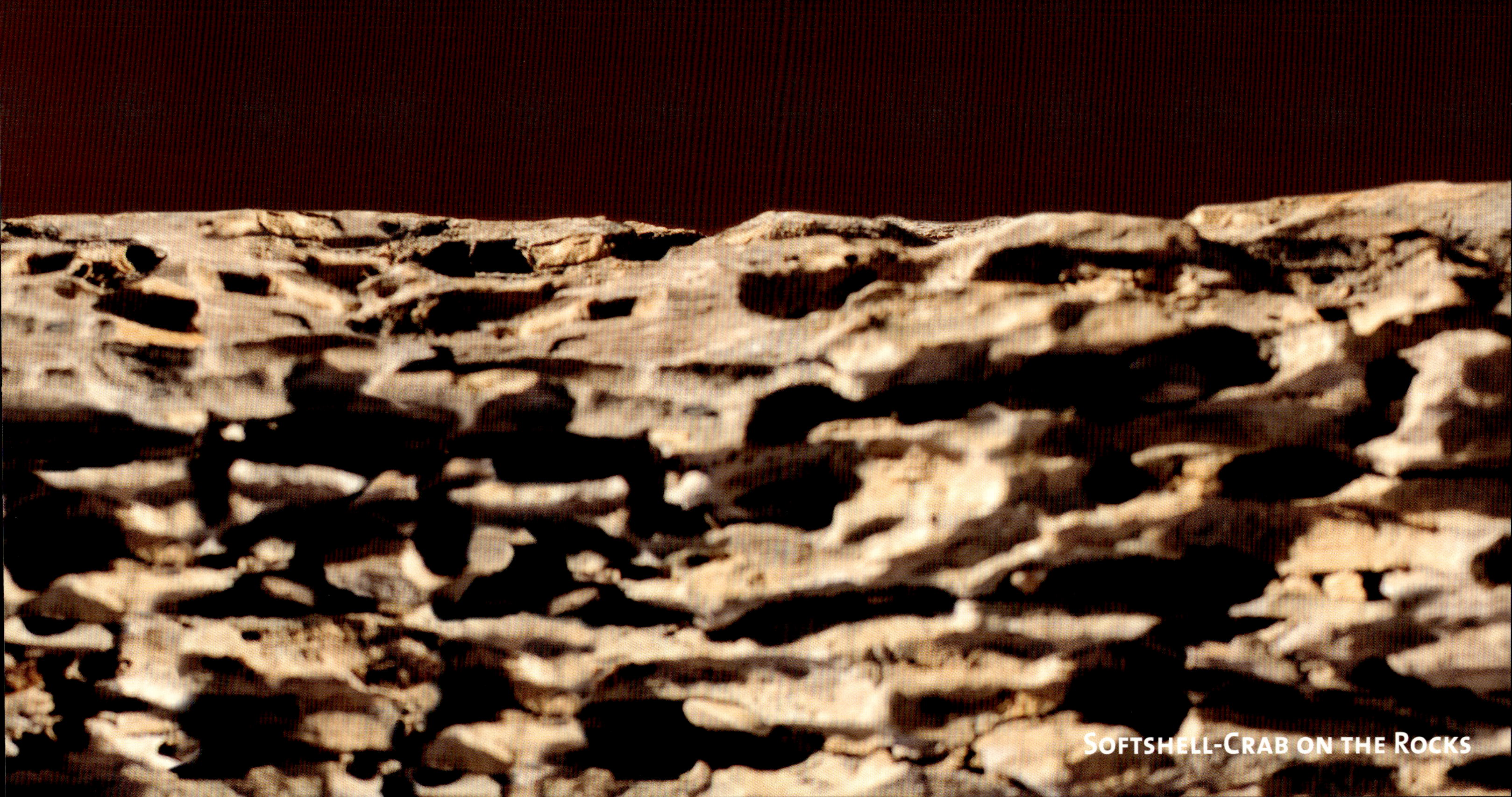

Softshell-Crab on the Rocks

Salmon-Tiger-Roll

Tuna Rose

Eyjafjallajökull Sushi

Stick o Tuna

Rainbow Sashimi

Spicy Devil

Super Crunchy Roll

Sushireis
8/12 Garnelen
Sushi Nori
Gurkenstreifen
Spicy-Sesam (gerösteter, gewürzter Sesam)

Super Crunchy Roll

sushi rice
prawns 8/12
nori
cucumber strips
spicy sesame seeds (roasted and seasoned)

Salmon Gold

Soceye-Lachs
Bund Schnittlauch
Sesamöl
Sojasauce
Sesam
Limonensauce
Blattgold

Salmon Gold

Soceye salmon
chive
sesame oil
soy sauce
sesame seeds
lemon juice
food gold leaf

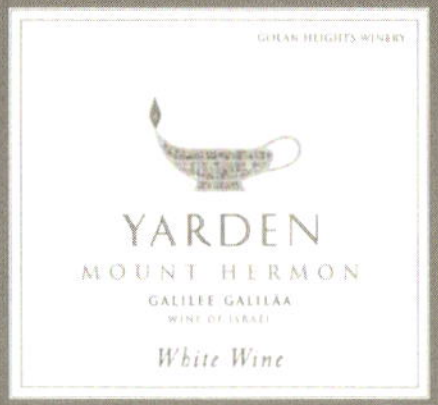

Kohl Roll

Wirsing
Hass-Avocado
in Ingwer eingelegte Gurken
Tamago
(japanisches Omelette)
Sushireis

Cabbage Roll

savoy cabbage
Hass avocado
pickled ginger cucumbers
tamago (japanese sweet egg omlette)
sushi rice

Lemon & Slice

Saint-Pierre-Fisch
Limetten-Sojaöl
rosa Pfeffer
Sakura-Kresse

Lemon & Slice

John Dory (St Peter's fish)
lime-infused soybean oil
pink peppercorns
Sakura cress

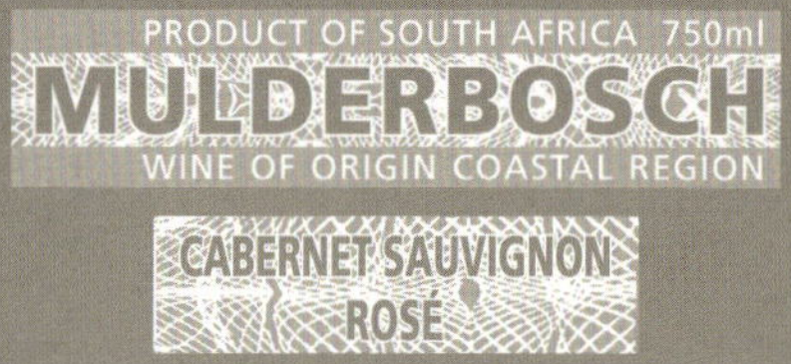

Beef Tataki

Rinderfilet
rosa Pfeffer
Chilisauce
Ponzu

Beef Tataki

lean beef fillet
pink peppercorns
chilli sauce
ponzu sauce (sourly soy sauce)

Salmon Dream Roll

Black-Tiger-Tempura (8/12)
Lachsfilet
Wasabi
Chilifäden
Sojasauce

Salmon Dream Roll

black tiger prawns (8/12)
salmon fillet
wasabi paste
chilli strings
soy sauce

East California Roll

Flusskrebs
Thai-Mango
Sushi-Reis
schwarzer Sesam Wasabi
Sakura-Kresse
Chili-Mayonnaise

East California Roll

crayfish
Thai mango
sushi rice
black sesame
wasabi paste
Sakura cress
chilli mayonnaise

Lobster Roll

Hummer
Sushi-Reis
Nori-Blätter
Gurkenstreifen
Wasabi
grüner Tee

Lobster Roll

lobster
sushi rice
nori
cucumber strips
wasabi paste
green tea

Crispy Ikarimi-Lachs

Ikarimi-Lachsfilet
Nori-Blätter
Tempura-Mehl
gebrannter Sauerrahm
Spicy-Sesam (gerösteter, gewürzter Sesam)
süße Sojasauce, frische Minze
getrocknete Orangenschalen

Crispy Ikarimi-Lachs

Ikarimi salmon
nori
tempura flour
smoked sour cream
spicy sesame seeds (roasted and seasoned)
sweet soy sauce, fesh mint leaves
orange peel

ROLLING Sauvignon Blanc Semillon
ALTHAUS
Ginseng Oolong Oriental

Turbot Black & White

Steinbuttfilet
Sushireis
Tobiko
Lauch
Orangen-Chili-Marinade
8 EL helle Sojasauce

Turbot Black & White

turbot
sushi rice
tobiko (flying fish roe)
leek
orange and chilli marinade
light soy sauce

Extra Cuvée de Réserve
Champagne
Pol Roger
Pure
Brut Nature

Duck-Tower

Pekingentenbrüste
Gurkenstreifen
Hoisin-Sauce
Sushireis

Duck-Tower

Peking roast duck breasts
strips of cucumber
hoisin sauce
sushi rice

BRANCAIA
TRE

Moonshadow

marinierte Pekingentenbrust
Hoisin-Sauce
(Pflaumensauce)
Sojasacue
Frühlingszwiebeln
Nori-Blätter „Gold“

Moonshadow

marinated Peking roast duck breasts
hoisin sauce
soy sauce
spring onions
nori „gold“

SILENI
Cellar Selection
Chardonnay
Hawke's Bay
Wine of New Zealand

Sliced Octopus

marinierter Oktopus
Pimentos
Schnittlauch
Gurkenstreifen
Ingwer-Soja-Marinade
Sushireis

Sliced Octopus

marinated octopus
pimiento chilli
chive
cucumber strips
ginger soy marinade
sushi rice

King's Sashimi

Hamachi-Filet
Meerrettich
Sourcreme
einige Flocken Maldon-Sea-Salz
Zitronengras-Gewürzsauce

King's Sashimi

hamachi fillet
horseradish
sour cream
maldon salt
lemongrass sauce

White Dream Roll

gekochte Garnelen
Avocado
Knoblauchkresse
frische Sahne

White Dream Roll

cooked large prawns
avocado
garlic cress
fresh cream

Spicy Rabbit Tiger Roll

Sushi-Reis
Thunfisch
Gurkenstreifen
gekochte Garnelen (ebi)
Chili-Mayonnaise
Sriracha (Chilisauce)

Spicy Rabbit Tiger Roll

sushi rice
thuna
cucumber strips
cooked large prawns
chilli mayonnaise
sriracha (chilli sauce)

Double-Smoke-Unagi Roll

gegrillter Aal
Gurkenstreifen
Nori-Blätter „Gold"
Sushi-Reis
Unagi-Sauce
(Unagi = japan. Aal)

Double-Smoke-Unagi Roll

grilled eel
cucumber strips
halved nori "gold"
sushi rice
unagi sauce
(unagi = jap. eel)

Loup de Green Roll

Filet vom Loup de Mer
Thai-Spargel
Frühlingszwiebeln
Sushireis
Spicy-Lemon-Sojasauce

Loup de Green Roll

Loup de Mer fillet
Thai asparagus
spring onions
sushi rice
spicy lemon and soy sauce

ALTHAUS
Lemon Gras Tea

Tandoori-Chicken
(India meets Hamburg)

mariniertes Tandoori-Hühnchen
Sushireis
Hass-Avocado
Rucola
Joghurt-Minze-Sauce

Tandoori-Chicken
(India meets Hamburg)

marinated tandoori chicken
sushi rice
Hass avocados
rocket
yoghurt and mint sauce

Wooden Cucumber
Tuna Sashimi

Mittelstück vom Thunfisch
Spicy-Sesam
Frischkäse
Gurkenstreifen
süße Sojasauce

Wooden Cucumber
Tuna Sashimi

tuna loin
spicy sesame seeds
(roasted and seasoned)
cream cheese
cucumber strips
sweet soy sauce

Sweet Crab Roll on Mozer's

Yellowfin-Thunfisch
Hass-Avocado
Minze
Nori-Blätter
Sushireis
Sojasauce

Sweet Crab Roll on Mozer's

Yellowfin tuna
Hass avocados
mint leaves
nori
sushi rice
soy sauce

SILENI
CELLAR SELECTION
SAUVIGNON BLANC
MARLBOROUGH
WINE OF NEW ZEALAND

Tobiko Point

Dorade Royal gegrillt
Olivenöl
Ponzu-Sauce
(säuerliche Sojasauce)
Tobiko-Wasabi
(Tobiko = Fliegenfisch-Kaviar)

Tobiko Point

grilled gilthead bream
olive oil
ponzu sauce
(sourly soy sauce)
tobiko wasabi
(tobiko = flying fish roe)

SILENI
CELLAR SELECTION
CHARDONNAY
HAWKE'S BAY
WINE OF NEW ZEALAND

Racasse Sashimi

Drachenkopf (Racasse)
roter Tobiko
Olivenöl
Ponzu-Sauce
(säuerliche Sojasauce)

Racasse Sashimi

scorpion fish (racasse)
red tobiko (flying fish roe)
olive oil
ponzu sauce
(sourly soy sauce)

MOSEL RIESLING
Wiltinger
ALTE REBEN
St. URBANS-HOF

Stuffed Salmon

Lachsscheiben
Sauerrahm
alter Balsamico
Schnittlauch

Stuffed Salmon

salmon slices
sour cream
old balsamic vinegar
chive

LOS VASCOS
CHARDONNAY

ALTHAUS
Milk Oolong Tea

Naked Salmon

Perigord-Lachs
Keta-Kaviar
Wasabi-Tobiko
Erdbeerminze

Naked Salmon

Perigord salmon
salmon caviar
wasabi tobiko (flying fish roe)
mentha species „strawberry“

Nepal History Roll

Rinderfilet
grüner Spargel
Hass-Avocado
Asia-Pesto
(geröstete Macadamia-Nüsse, Basilikum, Petersilie, Olivenöl)

Nepal History Roll

beef fillet
green asparagus
Hass avocado
asian pesto
(roasted macadamia nuts, basil, parsley, olive oil)

The Deep Red

Charolais-Rind
Nori-Blätter
Wasabi
dunkle Sojasauce
Frühlingszwiebeln

The Deep Red

Charolais beef
nori
wasabi paste
dark soy sauce
spring rolls

Khukuri Eel

gegrillter Aal
Tofu-Omlette
Unagi-Sauce
Schnittlauch

Khukuri Eel

grilled eel
tofu omlette
unagi sauce (unagi = jap. eel)
chive

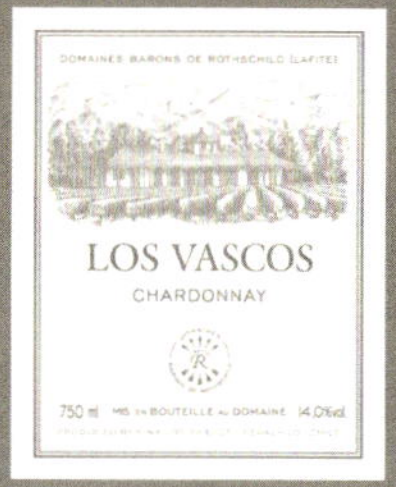

Mister Beef Roll

Rinderfilet
grüner Spargel
Chili-Sauce
Sushi-Reis

Mister Beef Roll

beef fillet
green asparagus
chilli sauce
sushi rice

ALTHAUS
Assam Melang Tea

Imprisoned Salmon Sashimi

Lachs-Sashimi
weißer Rettich
eingelegter Ingwer
Wasabi
helle Sojasauce

Imprisoned Salmon Sashimi

salmon sashimi
white raddish
pickled ginger
wasabi paste
light soy sauce

Deep Sea Roll

Big Eye Tuna
Hummer
Süßwassergarnelen
Hass-Avocado
Gurkenbrunoise
roter und grüner Tobiko
Schisokresse

Deep Sea Roll

Bigeye tuna
lobster
freshwater prawns
Hass avocado
cucumber brunoise
red and green tobiko (flying fish roe)
Shiso cress

ALTHAUS
Assam Melang Tea

Retro-Psychedelic-Sushi

Bananen
Tempurateig
Honig
Kokosflocken
Sushireis
Sojapapier

Retro-Psychedelic-Sushi

bananas
tempura flour
honey
grated coconut
sushi rice
sheets of soybean paper

Rabbit-Sushi

marinierte Erdbeeren
indische Mango
Nori-Blätter
Sushireis

Rabbit-Sushi

marinated strawberries
Indian mango
nori
sushi rice

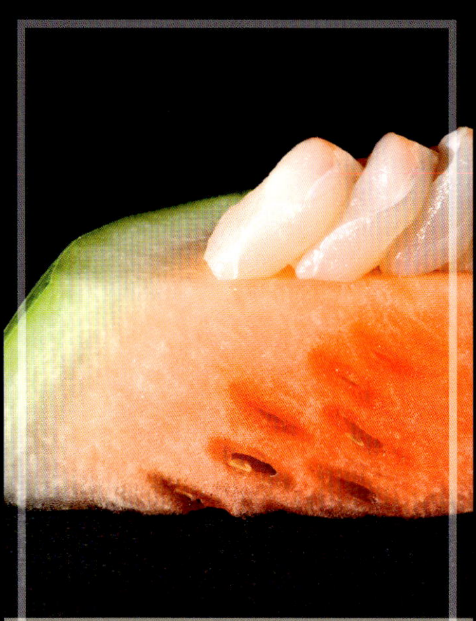

Watermelon Jacob

Loup de Mer-Filet
gegrillte Wassermelonen
chinesischer Lauch
Chili-Marinade

Watermelon Jacob

Loup de Mer fillet
grilled watermelon
Chinese leek
chilli marinade

Tea

Black Tuna on Green

Thunfisch
schwarzer Sesam
Teriyaki-Sauce

Black Tuna on Green

tuna fillet
black sesame seeds
teriyaki sauce

ALTHAUS

Bancha Rinji Yoru Tea

Salmon Dream Sashimi

schottischer Lachs
Sojasauce
Chili-Miso-Paste
Thai-Basilikum
Koriander
Nori-Blätter

Salmon Dream Sashimi

Scottish salmon
soy sauce
chilli and miso paste
Thai basil leaves
coriander leaves
nori

Mila Raper

getrocknete Tomaten
Hass-Avocado
Gurkenscheiben
Nori-Blätter
Sakura-Kresse

Mila Raper

dried tomatoes
Hass avocados
cucumber slices
nori
Sakura cress

Khampa-Beef-Sashimi

US-Beef
braune Butter
Sojasauce
Limonensaft
Schnittlauch
Feuer aus der Dose

Khampa-Beef-Sashimi

U.S. beef
brown butter
soy sauce
lemon juice
chive
tinned fire

Crazy Daisy Duck Roll

Barbarie-Entenbrust
Tempura-Teig
Gurkenstreifen
Frühlingszwiebeln
Sushireis

Crazy Daisy Duck Roll

Barbary duck breast
tempura flour
cucumber strips
spring onions
sushi rice

Brushed Mint-Chicken

Tandoori-Chicken
Koriander-Minze-Sauce

Brushed Mint-Chicken

tandoori chicken
coriander and mint sauce

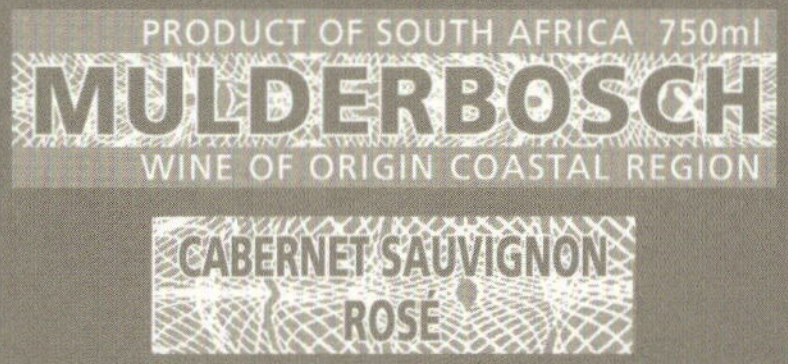

Softshell-Crab on the Rocks

Softshell-Crabs
Tempura-Mehl
schwarzer Tobiko
Gewürz-Sojasauce

Softshell-Crab on the Rocks

soft shell crabs
tempura flour
black tobiko (flying fish roe)
spicy soy sauce

Salmon-Tiger-Roll

gekochte Garnelen
Lachsscheiben
grüner Spargel
Schittlauch
Asia-Pesto
(Koriander, Sellerie, Thai-Basilikum, Chili, Ingwer, Traubenkernöl, Sesamöl)

Salmon-Tiger-Roll

cooked prawns
salmon slices
green asparagus
chive
Asian pesto
(coriander leaves, celery, Thai basil, chillies, ginger, grape seed oil, sesame oil)

Tuna Rose

Toro
(Thunfischbauch)

Tuna Rose

toro
(fatty belly meat of the tuna)

Eyjafjallajökull Sushi

Thai-Papaya
Thai-Mango
Mascarpone
Sushireis
Sojapapier
gehobelte Schokolade (80 %)

Eyjafjallajökull Sushi

Thai papaya
Thai mango
mascarpone
sushi rice
sheets of soybean paper
grated chocolate (80 %)

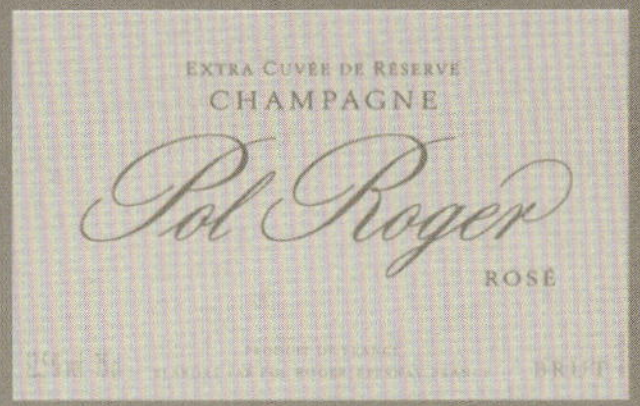

Stick o Tuna

Maguro (Thunfischfilet)
schwarzer Tobiko
(Fliegenfisch-Kaviar)
Teriyaki-Chili-Marinade

Stick o Tuna

maguro (bluefin tuna fillet)
black tobiko (flying fish roe)
teriyaki chilli marinade

Rainbow Sashimi

Thunfisch
Loup de Mer
schottischer Wildlachs
Zitronen- und Limonenzesten
Chilischotenstreifen
Sojasauce, Nussbutter
Chilisauce, Teriyaki-Sauce

Rainbow Sashimi

tuna
Loup de Mer
Scottish wild salmon
zest of lemons and limes
chilli strings
soy sauce, nut butter
chilli sauce, teriyaki sauce

Heavy Metal Sushi

Heilbuttfilet
Butter
Zitronen
Frühlingszwiebeln
marinierte Tomaten
(oder: süße Paprika)

Heavy Metal Sushi

halibut
butter
lemons
spring onions
marinated tomatoes
(alternatively sweet peppers)

Spicy Devil

Negitoro
Sushireis
Gurkenstreifen
Nori-Blätter
rote Chilischoten
Knoblauch-Chilipaste

Spicy Devil

negitoro
sushi rice
cucumber strips
nori
red chillies
garlic and chilli paste

Sencha Senpai Tea

„Kulinarik – das Herz des Hauses“

Imposant. Außergewöhnlich. Ein bisschen majestätisch. Einfach anders. Das ist das seit 2004 bestehende *east* im Szenestadtteil St.Pauli. In jeder Hinsicht: ‚Europe meets Asia. Crossover. Top-Class. Different Styles. Fusion of Cultures' – an diesen selbst formulierten Ambitionen messen sich die Macher des *east* und ihr Team stets aufs Neue. Dafür ist das *east* multikonzeptionell: Restaurant, Bar, Lounge. Und ein Hotel ist es natürlich auch, der zurückhaltende Anspruch wird durch den Satz „You can even sleep if you want“ deutlich. Doch angesichts der kulinarischen Köstlichkeiten könnte man das Schlafen fast vergessen. Im *east* steht die gastronomische Kompetenz im Vordergrund, die sich, dem Namen verpflichtet, nach Osten, nach Asien orientiert. „Mit den USA bringe ich Geschwindigkeit und fettes Essen in Verbindung, mit Asien Gesundheit, warme Farben und gutes Essen“, sagt Christoph Strenger, einer der beiden Geschäftsführer des *east*. Konzeptionell und architektonisch sollte hierfür eine Symbiose gefunden werden.

Die alte Eisengießerei, die nur einen Steinwurf von der Reeperbahn entfernt ist und viele Jahre leer stand, war von Anfang an als Standort für dieses Ziel ideal. Als die beiden Hamburger Top-Gastronomen Christoph Strenger und Marc Ciunis vor fast zehn Jahren vor dem verfallenen Gebäude standen, wussten sie: Daraus kann man etwas Tolles machen. Für ambitionierte Pläne dieser Größenordnung haben beide ein professionelles Gespür. Strenger entwirft seit 1989 Gastronomie- und Foodservice-Konzepte, seinem Unternehmen Gastro Consulting mit rund 800 Mitarbeitern, das er zusammen mit seinen Partnern Roland Koch und Michael Maier führt, gehören heute 22 Betriebe, darunter mehrere Bolero-Restaurants, das Herzblut auf der Reeperbahn, das Paulaner's in Bremen und als jüngstes Projekt der Chilli-Club in der neuen Hamburger Hafencity. Marc Ciunis wollte eigentlich Koch werden, arbeitete aber im Restaurant Landhaus Scherrer in Hamburg zunächst im Service als Restaurantfachmann, ging dann nach Sylt und arbeitete in der Barlegende Karlchen Rosenzweig. Fünf Jahre später kehrte er nach Hamburg zurück und machte sich mit der Intelligent Drinking Company, der ersten Hamburger Cocktailschule, selbstständig. Es folgten das legändere Cenario in Eppendorf, das 1996 Bar des Jahres wurde, und schließlich die Eröffnung des CIU' am Ballindamm. Fast nebenbei hat Marc Ciunis heute sehr bekannte Cocktails erfunden: Ipanema, Passionata, Prince und Cassidy's Cane gehen auf seine Karte. Und heute führen Strenger und Ciunis als Geschäftsführer das *east*. „Dabei wollte ich nie einen Laden auf dem Kiez aufmachen!“, gesteht Marc Cuinis. „Aber die Herausforderung und die Aussicht auf etwas Außergewöhnliches waren zu groß. Allerdings sind wir Gastronomen, von Hotelerie hatten wir keine Ahnung.“ So kam Anne-Marie Bauer ins Boot. Die gebürtige Niederbayerin war bereits über viele Jahre sehr erfahren in der Hotelerie, darunter mit Projekten in der Schweiz und im Jemen, und betreute von Beginn an das ambitionierte Hotelkonzept. Sehr erfolgreich, wie sich schnell zeigte. Heute ist Bauer die Direktorin des Hauses. „Die beste Fachfrau in der Branche“, wie Ciunis betont. Eine echte Konkurrenz gab es für das *east* nicht. „Außerdem,“ so ist Ciunis überzeugt, „haben wir in Hamburg zwar eine große Dichte privater Hotels. Aber wir sind untereinander ganz hanseatisch: Es gibt keine Konkurrenz, sondern einen großen Austausch.“

„The Kitchen – the Heart of the House“

Impressive. Unusual. Nearly majestic. Simply different. That's how it is. Since 2004, east is located in the hip district of St. Pauli. „Europe meets Asia. Top-class. Different styles. Fusion of cultures.“ The creators of east and their team continually measure themselves with what is new. The east is multi conceptual: restaurant, bar, lounge. And, it goes without saying, a hotel. The modest claim evidenced in the sentence: „you can even sleep if you want,“ makes it clear. Considering the culinary delicacies you could pretty much forget about sleeping. In east, gastronomical competence stands in the foreground, and, as the name implies, is oriented toward Asia. „The association I make with the U.S., is speed and fatty foods, whereas with Asia one thinks of health, warm colors, and good food,“ says Christoph Strenger, one of the managers of east. The aim is to create a symbiosis between the conceptual and the architectural elements.

The old iron foundry that's only a stone's throw away from the Reeperbahn and has been empty for years, turned out to be the ideal location for this purpose from the very beginning. When the two Hamburg top gastronomes Christoph Strenger and Marc Ciunis stood in front of the derelict building nearly ten years ago, they knew: With this location we can do something great. Both of them have a professional intuition for ambitious plans of that dimension. Since 1989 Strenger is designing gastronomic and food-service concepts. He runs Gastro Consulting, a company with approximately 800 staff members, along with his partners Roland Koch and Michael Maier. Today they run 22 other businesses, including a number of Bolero Restaurants, the soul of the Reeperbahn, the Paulaner's in Bremen and, their most recent project, the Chilli-Club in Hamburg's new Port City. Marc Ciunis originally wanted to be a cook, but worked initially as a restaurant specialist in the service sector at Landhaus Scherrer in Hamburg, followed by his move to Sylt, where he worked for the legendary Karlchen Rosenzweig Bar. Five years later he returned to Hamburg and together with the Intelligent Drinking Company, he set up the first independent cocktail school. This was followed by the legendary Cenario Bar in Eppendorf, that in 1996 was nominated Bar of the Year, and finally, he opened the CIU' on Ballindamm. In addition to that, Marc Ciunis has invented famous cocktails such as Ipanema, Passionata, Prince and Cassidy's Cane. And today, Strenger and Ciunis manage the restaurant east. „Actually I never wanted to open a business in that neighborhood,“ admits Marc Ciunis. „But I couldn't deprive myself of the challenge and the prospects of creating something exceptional. Nevertheless we're gastronomes, we knew nothing about the hotel business.“ That is why Anne-Marie Bauer jumped on board. Born in Lower Bavaria she had already acquired many years of experience in the hotel business, including projects in Switzerland and Yemen, and from the very beginning took charge of the ambitious hotel concept. Very successfully so, as became quickly apparent. Today, Bauer is the director of the house. „The best specialist in the field“ emphasizes Ciunis. There has never been a serious competitor for east. „Besides,“ Ciunis is convinced, „in Hamburg we have a dense concentration of private hotels, but among ourselves we're Hanseatic in nature: There's no real competition, just a generous exchange.“

Von Anfang an gab es für das *east* nur ein Marketing-Konzept: das außergewöhnliche Design, verwirklicht vom Stararchitekten Jordan Mozer. „Fernöstlichen Charme mit westlicher Industriegeschichte zu verknüpfen und ein cross-kulturelles Gesamtkunstwerk zu schaffen“, erklärt Christoph Strenger die damals gesetzten Ziele. Mit Jordan Mozer holte man den Perfektionisten ins Boot. „Räume müssen dich glücklich machen. Lebendig und menschlich werden sie durch die perfekte Verbindung von Funktionalität, Intuition und Emotion“, beschreibt Mozer sein Arbeitscredo, das ihn international so gefragt sein lässt. Diese Handschrift, an der auch Christoph Strenger selbst mitgeschrieben hat (er entwarf u.a. die Yakshi's Bar), ist im *east* überall zu sehen: Einige Etagen sind von poppigen Farben geprägt, andere halten sich mit dezenten Farben zurück und bringen die eher gemütliche, also chillige Note. Die östlichen Reminiszenzen, auch mit Anleihen aus dem Feng Shui, sind unverkennbar, variieren aber gekonnt mit industriellem Backstein und brechen Sehgewohnheiten auf. Statt asiatischer Kitsch-Accessoires bilden Designelemente mit geschwungenen und organischen Formen von Jordan Mozer Akzente und entspannen das Auge. Dominiert wird das Ensemble von den stilisierten Wabenwänden, die die Schwere hoher Wände aufzulösen scheinen, und von den vier imposanten Säulen, die wirken, als seien sie mit Falten werfenden Satinstoffen überzogen. Sie verbinden das Restaurant mit der Bar und den Lounges. Jede Etage hat einen eigenen Stil, eine eigene Farbe, einen eigenen asiatischen Duft: Ginger, Cinnamon, Lotus oder Mandarin. Verläuft man sich, folgt man dem Duft. Alle Details, vom Türgriff über das geschwungene Waschbecken bis hin zu den avantgardistischen Lampen wurden für das *east* entworfen.

Hamburger Hafen, Kiez, Bordsteinschwalben, City, Musical, Hafen, St.Pauli-Stadion, Schanze – alles ist um die Ecke und bilden ein Gesamtensemble, das Hamburger wie Gäste der Stadt anzieht. Nachts, vor allem am Wochenende, treffen Hamburger Partyvolk und Prominenz, Lifestyle und Business auf internationale Gäste und nehmen an der Yakshi's Bar, in der Smirnoff-Lounge oder im Dedon Island einen Drink, Cocktail, Wein oder Champagner. Oder tanzen im Club ‚uppereast‘ vor riesigen multifunktionellen, in allen erdenklichen Farben blinkenden LED-Bildschirmen. Gespielt wird Chill-out und Elektro-Pop, vor allem von CDs, die vom eigenen east-Label produziert und von DJ Ping zusammengestellt und gemixt werden. „Professionell, freundschaftlich, familiär. Unsere Gäste sollen sich wie Freunde fühlen“, sagt Direktorin Anne-Marie Bauer. „Und wir versuchen, unsere Gäste jedes Jahr mit einem neuen Highlight zu überraschen.“ Deswegen gibt es noch mehr: Einen Tagungsbereich mit kombinierbaren Räumen, einen ausgedehnten Sport- und Wellnessbereich (ebenfalls von Mozer entworfen), Massage- und Beautyabteilung, ein kleines Kino, in dem während der Fußball-Weltmeisterschaft 2010 die deutschen Spiele gezeigt wurden. Und in der ‚east private kitchen‘, dessen Interieur von Anne-Marie Bauer ausgesucht wurde, kann man auf 135 Quadratmetern in einer hochmodernen Küche mit Freunden kochen oder sich bekochen lassen und anschließend auch noch schlafen.

Die Auszeichnungen für das außergewöhnliche Interieur und Gastro-Konzept häufen sich: European Hotel Design Award, Hamburger Gründerpreis 2006, Golden Key

From the very beginning there was only one marketing concept for east: a unique design, realized by star architect Jordan Mozer. „To combine Far Eastern charm with Western industrial history and create a cross cultural artistic synthesis of the two,“ explains Christoph Strenger, referring to the goals he set for himself at that time. With Jordan Mozer, a perfectionist was brought on board. „The rooms have to make you feel happy. Through the perfect relationship between functionality, intuition and emotion it acquires a more lively and human feel,“ describes Mozer his work credo, that has made him so popular internationally. His signature, co-written by Christoph Strenger (he designed the Yakshi Bar, among others), is visibly present everywhere you look in east: A number of the floors are dominated by jazzy colors, others are more subtle and contribute to a more comfortable relaxed atmosphere. The Eastern influence, borrowing also from Feng Shui, is unmistakable and diversified with the skillful introduction of industrial brick, breaking old ways of looking at things. Instead of Asiatic kitsch accessories, design elements with contoured and organic forms from Jordan Mozer set the tone and relax the eye. The ensemble is dominated by stylized honeycombed walls, that appear to dissolve the heavy high walls, and from the four imposing columns, that seem to be draped in satin. They connect the restaurant with the bar and lounges. Every floor has its own style, its distinct color, its particular Asian fragrance: ginger, cinnamon, lotus or mandarin. If you lose your way, just follow the scent. Every single detail was specially designed for east, from the door handle to the curved wash basins, and the avant-garde lamps.

Hamburg harbor, the neighborhood, streetwalkers, downtown, musicals, the port, St. Pauli Stadium, the Schanze district – everything is just around the corner, creating a complete package that attracts the residents as well as the visitors. At night, above all on weekends, party goers and celebrities, lifestyle and business people mingle with international guests and partake of a drink, a cocktail, wine or champagne at the Yakshi's Bar, in the Smirnoff-Lounge or in Dedon Island. Or go dancing in the Club uppereast in front of giant multi-functioning LED screens, blinking in every conceivable color. Chill-Out and Electric Pop is played, for the most part from CDs, that are produced by east's own label and arranged and mixed by Dj Ping. „Professional, amicable, informal. Our guests should have the feeling they're our friends,“ says director Anne-Marie Bauer. „And we try to surprise our friends every year with some new highlight.“ And there is even more: A conference area allowing any number of arrangements, an extensive sports and wellness center (likewise designed by Mozer), a massage and beauty department, a small cinema, in which you could view the German team in competition during the world championship of 2010. And in east's private kitchen, whose interior was especially designed by Anne-Marie Bauer, friends can cook for friends in an ultramodern kitchen, occupying 135 square meters, and afterwards use the sleeping accommodations.

The commendation for this exceptional interior and culinary concept are piling up: European Hotel Design Award, Hamburger Gründerpreis 2006, Golden Key Award for the second most beautiful Design Hotel in the world, the Golden Palm of the

Award als zweitschönstes Designhotel der Welt, Goldene Palme des Leaders Club, AIT Award 2005, um nur die wichtigsten zu nennen. Für dieses preisgekrönte Gesamtkonzept gab es Vorbilder: „Wir waren zwar von den Buddha-Bars inspiriert, aber wir wollten natürlich keinen Abklatsch", erzählt Christoph Strenger. „Mozer ist das beeindruckend gelungen. Das, was im *east* am meisten auffällt, nämlich die Säulen und die Wände, sind seine Ideen." Dominieren in den Buddha-Bars die Buddha-Statuen, sind es im *east* diese besonderen architektonischen Elemente. Das ist das Einzigartige. Außerdem war man von den Ideen eines Ian Schrager beeindruckt, dem die Erfindung und Entwicklung der sogenannten Boutique-Hotels zugeschrieben wird und schon damals seine Hotels vom französischen Designer Philippe Starck kreieren ließ. Doch die Macher des *east* holen sich vor allem durch Reisen Inspirationen und Ideen für neue Konzepte. Kürzlich reisten sie zusammen nach Kuala Lumpur, Singapur, Tokyo und Shanghai. Christoph Strenger: „Für mich ist es Teil meiner Arbeit, durch die Welt zu reisen, mich in New York oder Las Vegas umzusehen – oder auch Kochbücher zu lesen."

Das *east* ist ohne Zweifel das Flaggschiff der gastronomischen Projekte. Doch neue warten. In Kooperation mit dem Kultrestaurant Sansibar auf Sylt entstehen 2011 Dependancen auf Mallorca im Port Adriano, „dem Hafen für Yachten, die in Palma keinen Platz haben", lacht Ciunis. ‚harbour*east*' wird der Ableger heißen, den Philippe Starck entwickelt. Auch in der neuen Hamburger Hafencity teilen sich das *east* und die Sansibar eine Location in bester Lage vor den Marco Polo Terrassen: Unten wird die ‚Sansibar Weinbar' untergebracht sein, oben das ‚east Harbour'. Auf Mallorca wird es umgekehrt sein. Doch eine Kopie des *east* in Hamburg kann es nicht geben. „Mit neuen Konzepten muss ich nicht das *east* toppen", sagt Christoph Strenger. „Das *east* ist ein Glücksfall für die Gastronomie, das aber auch viel Aufwand erfordert hat. Hamburg und Mallorca sind für mich aber beides Heimat."

Sushi als Corporate Identity

Als gastronomischer Glücksfall hat sich vor allem das Sushi der beiden Meister Ngima Sherpa und Tamatsu Tashi erwiesen. Denn die runden Formen, das chillige Ambiente mit asiatischem Flair werden durch die kulinarischen Hochgenüsse bestens ergänzt. Sushi sollte von Anfang an die Corporate Identity sein, etwas, das die Gäste mit dem *east* verbinden und in einem Atemzug nennen. Christoph Strenger nennt es das ‚Burning Desire of Return', das brennende Verlangen also, immer wieder zurückkommen zu wollen. Das hat er selbst an den verschiedensten Orten der Welt erlebt und beschreibt es als ein beglückendes Gefühl. „Und damit wollen wir weg vom klassischen Sushi, wollen phantasievolle neue Kreationen, mit neuen hochwertigen Produkten. Und der Erfolg gibt uns recht: Wir können Menschen begeistern, die eigentlich keinen Fisch essen." Mit Ngima Sherpa und Tamatsu Tashi seien dafür zwei Spitzenleute gefunden worden. „Ngima und Tamatsu prägen einen ganz entscheidenden Teil der Kulinarik in unserem Haus. Die Kulinarik ist schließlich das Herz des Hauses!" Sushi sei außerdem auch immer eine Vertrauenssache, betont Strenger: „Wir haben es mit rohem Fisch zu tun, da ist Hygiene ganz besonders wichtig. Dieses hohe Vertrauen genießen die Jungs ohne Zweifel. Und das Buch ist eine schöne Visitenkarte für unser Haus, aber auch für die Sushi-Meister." Die Frische der Fische und Meeresfrüchte steht natürlich ebenfalls im Vordergrund. Da ruft der Großhändler auch schon mal

Leaders Club, AIT Award 2005, only to mention the most important. There were role models for this award winning package: „We were inspired by the Buddha-Bars, but naturally we didn't want to make a cheap imitation," says Christoph Strenger. „And Mozer has impressively succeeded. In east, the first things to grab your attention, namely the columns and the walls, are his idea." Just like the Buddha statues dominate the Buddha bars, east is defined by its special architectural elements. That's what represents the uniqueness of east. Besides, everybody was very impressed by the ideas of Jan Schrager, who is credited for inventing and developing the so-called Boutique-Hotels and who already at that time had his hotels styled by the French designer Philippe Starck. But the makers of east gather their inspiration and ideas for new concepts mainly by travelling throughout the world. Quite recently they traveled together to Kuala Lumpur, Singapore, Tokyo and Shanghai. „I feel it is part of my work to travel the world, to browse around New York or Las Vegas – or just look at cookbooks," Christoph Strenger states.

Without a doubt east is the flagship of their gastronomic projects. But there are others waiting. In cooperation with the legendary cult-restaurant ‚Sansibar' on Sylt, subsidiaries will emerge in 2011 in Mallorca, Port Adriano, „the port for yachts that have no space in Palma", Ciunis laughs. The subsidiary, designed by Philipp Starck, will be called ‚harboureast'. east and ‚Sansibar' also share the prime location of the Marco Polo Terraces in the new Hamburg Hafencity. The ‚Sansibar Winebar' will occupy the lower floor, with ‚harboureast' being situated above. In Mallorca it will be the other way around. But don't expect a copy of east in Hamburg. „I don't have to upstage east, trying to come up with new concepts," says Christoph Strenger. east is a stroke of luck for the gastronomy, but it also took a lot of effort. Now I call both Hamburg and Mallorca my home."

Sushi as Corporate Identity

The sushi created by the two masters Ngima Sherpa and Tamatsu Tashi has turned out to be a gastronomical windfall. The rounded shapes in the interior architecture, and the relaxed ambience with an Asiatic flair are perfectly complemented by the culinary treat. From the beginning, sushi was intended to be their Corporate Identity, something the guests could associate with east and mention in the same breath. Christoph Strenger calls it the „Burning Desire of Return," the burning desire to come back time and time again. It's something he experienced himself throughout his travels around the world and he describes it as a delightful experience. „And that's why we want to get away from classic sushi – we want new imaginative creations with top quality products. And success proves us right: We can get people excited who don't even eat fish." With the discovery of Ngima Sherpa and Tamatsu Tashi they have found two top men in the field that can do just that. „Ngima and Tamatsu play a very crucial role in the culinary sector of our business. In the end, the kitchen is the heart of the house! Apart from that," Strenger emphasizes, „sushi is also always a matter of trust. We are dealing with raw fish, that makes hygiene a top priority. Without a doubt the two of them relish this high level of trust. And the book is not only a nice calling card for our house, but also for the sushi chefs." Of course the freshness of the fish and seafood has the highest priority. It might easily happen, that the wholesale dealer calls and offers a 120 kilo halibut. „We always want to know exactly,

Snacks

an und bietet einen 120 Kilogramm schweren Heilbutt an. „Wir wollen immer genau wissen, woher der Fisch kommt", sagt Marc Ciunis. „Aber wir können uns auch auf unsere Händler verlassen." Zudem gibt es etwa alle sechs Wochen ein Testessen. Vertrauen ist gut, Kontrolle noch besser.

Doch die feinen Speisen alleine sind es nicht, die das besondere Flair des Restaurants prägen. Das ‚Food-Sharing-System' sorgt zudem für Geselligkeit asiatischer Art. Marc Ciunis, der auch den F&B-Bereich zusammen mit dem F&B-Manager Christopher Weckler betreut, erklärt, worum es dabei geht: „Deutsche neigen dazu, ihre Hauptspeise selbst zu essen. Wir möchten unsere Gäste dazu animieren, es den Asiaten gleich zu tun und die Speisen zwar gemeinsam zu bestellen, aber untereinander zu teilen, von jedem etwas zu probieren. Das erhöht das Geschmackserlebnis."

Genießer sind sie natürlich alle, sonst würden sie erstens nicht in der Branche arbeiten und wären zweitens nicht so erfolgreich damit. Jeder hat seine eigenen Vorlieben: Anne-Marie Bauer liebt die bodenständige Küche, Eintopf, Rouladen, Sauerbraten, vor allem die bayerische Küche. Und ohne Schnittlauch geht gar nichts. „Kochen ist Genuss, eine Flasche Wein dazu, herrlich!" Und obwohl sie aus Bayern kommt, gesteht sie: „Ich wollte schon immer am Meer wohnen. Und in Hamburg ist das ja fast der Fall." Marc Ciunis ist ein Freund von Spargel, schön knackig, mit Parmesan, dazu Olivenöl und Meersalz, „am besten ‚garniert' mit einem halben Hähnchen", lacht er. Christoph Strenger haben es die Italiener angetan: Vitello Tonnato! Antipasti! Dazu einen Sauvignon Blanc oder einen guten Riesling. Aber auch die thailändische Küche gehört zu seinen Favoriten, genauso wie die chinesische und japanische. Er bleibt Asien eben treu. Aber er gesteht: „Essengehen gibt mir am meisten Inspiration, mehr, als selbst am Herd zu stehen." Und fügt schmunzelnd hinzu: „Im Herzen aber bin ich eigentlich Koch."

where the fish comes from," says Marc Ciunis, „and we can fully rely on our dealers." Moreover, they hold a test-meal approximately every six weeks. Trust is good, but control is better.

But it's not only the delicious food that characterizes the special atmosphere of the restaurant. The traditional ‚Food Sharing System' provides a distinctive Asian sociability. Marc Ciunis, who also supervises the F&B department together with manager Christoph Weckler explains, what this implies: „Germans tend not to share their main dish. We want to encourage our guests to emulate the Asian style, order together, share the dishes and try a little of everything. That contributes to the intensity of the taste experience."

Of course they are all connoisseurs, otherwise they wouldn't be working in this business in the first place, and secondly, not be so successful at it. Each of them has his own preferences: Anne-Marie Bauer loves down-to-earth cuisine, German stew, Beef Roulade, Sauerbraten (marinated roast) and, above all, Bavarian cooking. And nothing goes without chives. „Cooking is a great pleasure! And with a bottle of wine, what could be better!" And despite her Bavarian background she confesses: „I always wanted to live by the sea. And in Hamburg that's almost the case." Marc Ciunis is fond of asparagus, pleasantly crisp, with parmesan cheese, olive oil and sea salt, „at best ‚garnished' with half a fried chicken", he chuckles. Christoph Strenger fancies the Italian kitchen: Vitello Tonnato! Antipasti! Along with it a Sauvignon Blanc or a good Riesling. Thai cuisine also ranks among his favorites as well as the cuisine of China and Japan. In the end he remains faithful to Asia. But he confesses: „Dining out gives me the most inspiration, even more than standing at the stove myself. But deep in my heart I am a cook!", he adds with a smile.

S.PELLEGRI
EAST

EAST

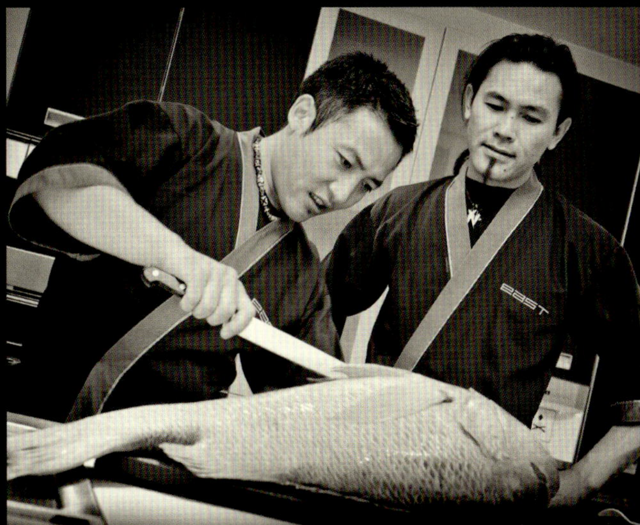
EAST

EAST

EAST

EAST
EAST

Oben (v.l.): Christopher Weckler, Ngima Sherpa, Anja Mönnich, Marc Ciunis, Tamatsu Tashi
Unten (v.l.): Christoph Strenger, Kathrin Beulshausen, Tell Wagner, Lutz Jäkel

Distribution by Neuer Umschau Buchverlag GmbH, Neustadt an der Weinstraße

The recipes in this book have been carefully tested by the author. The publishers and the author have made every effort to ensure that the recipes are accurate and safe but cannot accept liability for any resulting injury or loss or damage to property whether direct or consequential.

Recipes
Tamatsu Tashi and Ngima Sherpa, Hamburg
www.east-hamburg.de

Texts and photography
Lutz Jäkel, Hamburg
www.lutz-jaekel.com

Translation
Signe Mähler and William Cody Maher, Heidelberg

Foodstyling
Anja Mönnich, Hamburg
www.soul-of-food.de

Design and layout
Kaisers Ideenreich, Neustadt an der Weinstraße
www.kaisers-ideenreich.de

Reproduction
Lutz Jäkel and Kaisers Ideenreich

Overall production
NINO Druck GmbH, Neustadt an der Weinstraße
www.ninodruck.de

Printed and bound in Germany

ISBN: 978-3-86528-714-4

Visit our website: www.umschau-buchverlag.de

Special thanks for supporting this project so much and for making it possible to:

Timo Wolff (Fa. CWD); Lina Chormanskyte (Restaurant Manager east); Tell Wagner (Executive Chef east); Kathrin Beulshausen (Public Relations east); Anja Mönnich (Foodstyling); Lutz Jäkel (Photography); Daniel Schmidtholz (Fa. Althaus); Norbert Rosen (Nestlé Waters AG); Christopher Weckler (F&B Manager east); Yoshiko Ueno Müller (Premiumsake); Petra Mommens (Sommelier LOUIS C. JACOB); Oliver Thieme (Fa. CWD) and Thomas Kreye, Jan Töben, Anne Marie Bauer and Bianca Plettke.